Daniel Therriault

Battery

(a love story)

BROADWAY PLAY PUBLISHING INC
New York
www.broadwayplaypublishing.com
info@broadwayplaypublishing.com

BATTERY

Copyright © 1983, 1986

All rights reserved. This work is fully protected under the copyright laws of the United States of America.

No part of this publication may be photocopied, reproduced, stored in a retrieval system, or transmitted, in any form or by any means, electronic, mechanical, recording, or otherwise without the prior permission of the publisher.

Written permission is required for live performance of any sort. This includes readings, cuttings, scenes, and excerpts. For amateur and stock performances, please contact Broadway Play Publishing, Inc.

For all other rights, please contact William Craver, Writers and Artists Agency, 19 West 44th Street, #1000, New York, NY 10036-5903, 212-391-1112.

ISBN: 0-88145-003-0
First printing: February 1983
Second printing: January 1987
Third printing: August 1997
Cover art by Steve Mellor
Design by Marie Donovan

To Alison

BATTERY was originally produced Off-Off-Broadway in New York City by Theatre at St. Clement's, Michael Hadge, Artistic Director, through a special grant provided by the Barrie A. and Deedee Wigmore Foundation, on June 4, 1981. It was directed by George Ferencz, assisted by B. David Green. The setting and lights were designed by Peter Harrison, costumes by Sally J. Lesser, and the production stage manager was Virlana Tkacz, with the following cast, in order of appearance:

STAN.............................Stephen Mellor
RIP..............................Fritz Sperberg
BRANDY...........................Holly Hunter

The entire action occurs in Rip's Electric, a home appliance repair shop located in Chicago, Illinois.

The time is the present.

The action occurs within the period of three weeks.

Cast of Characters

RIP, owner of the shop
STAN, his apprentice
BRANDY, his girlfriend

ACT ONE

Scene 1

(Morning. The beginning of a work day. Rip's Electric is a various collection of broken household appliances: defective irons, lamps with shorts, and toasters that do not toast. If it is electric, it can stop working, and if it can stop working, it can be found in the shop. There are things that can only be described as gizmos and watchamacallits, and these, too, are broken. One door leads to the outside, the other to the washroom, and there is at least one window. A large worktable and drafting desk with chairs are used for repair and design, respectively.

RIP hums with the animal joy of being alive. He is an ace electrician and designer. The center of his being is electricity, and this voltage bolts and crackles into everything and everyone he touches. When he enters a room, people are attracted to him like a magnet thrown onto a heap of nails.

The brightness of STAN's character turns dark in the click of a light switch. He can be physically active, then suddenly slow moving, giggling one moment, frightened the next. He is an emotional roller coaster with RIP at the controls.

Both RIP and STAN wear dull-colored work clothes. RIP'S ELECTRIC is emblazoned onto each of their shirts.

STAN is found in the workshop. He blends in quite naturally in this room of dysfunction, as if he is just one more broken gadget. When STAN moves, it becomes clear that he is human. Coffee is perking in an electric coffeepot; he wraps a section of the percolator cord with electrical tape, gets shocked and jumps. He unplugs the cord. The coffeepot goes off. He finishes taping the cord and replugs it. The coffeepot turns on and continues to perk. STAN *stares vacantly at the pot.* RIP *enters vibrantly.* STAN *becomes instantly excited.*)

RIP: The night was a fight, a sad sight was my plight, but I gained height like a kite, when I plugged tight with my might!

STAN: You scored!

RIP: Like a stallion to stud.

BOTH: (*Singing*) That pal o' mine, oh, he's a palomino! (*They laugh.*)

RIP: I caught her in my sights at ten o'clock last night at Fatrack's Bar. Took aim at the target, tugged at the trigger, and fired at her with a sloe gin fizz. Shot myself up with a shooter. The bartender hit her with the bullet. I made my mark. I was sitting next to her. In like Flynn.

STAN: What she look like?

RIP: Perfection. Fresh off the assembly line. Her chrome shone. Fire-engine redhead. Not a dent in her fenders. Not a scratch on her doors. Her exhaust was sweet. Pure premium. I was getting high from the smell of her gasoline. And she was sooooo young.

STAN: So what happened?

RIP: You want me to tell the story?

STAN: Yeah.

RIP: Then let me tell the story.

STAN: Right.

RIP: Alright?

STAN: Alright.

RIP: Alright. (*Pause*) So I'm revving like a tuned engine in neutral, right? I grease her with another

ACT ONE

sloe gin. I'm getting oiled with my own shots. What does she say?

STAN: Your place or mine?

RIP: Jesus H. Am I describing a crass lady to you?

STAN: No.

RIP: Pay attention. I'm talking about a classy chassis.

STAN: Right.

RIP: She looks at me dreamy-like and says, 'Your eyes are as deep and clear as a Minnesota lake. I want to take off all my clothes and skinny-dip in them.'

STAN: In your eyes?

RIP: In my eyes. No clothes.

STAN: She said that?

RIP: Did I just say she said that?

STAN: Yeah you said she said that.

RIP: Then she said that.

STAN: She said that?

RIP: She said that. Where's my coffee?

STAN: Perking. I fixed the wire.

RIP: Tape the short?

STAN: Yeah.

RIP: Get shocked?

STAN: Yeah.

RIP: Get the morning paper?

STAN: (*Indicating the newspaper.*) Yeah. So what happened?

RIP: I cruise over to her place. My wheels, her pad. Right?

STAN: Check.

RIP: Rule number one: When humping a bumper?

BOTH: Pump your brains out.

RIP: Rule number two.

BOTH: Plug's pulled, light's out.

RIP: You make your getaway. If you stay with a woman after, it's like flooding your engine. You must maintain. Plug's pulled, you leave.

STAN: Check.

RIP: A chick is like your key to the ignition. You stick her in the drive shaft, she cranks the motor, gets you where you're going, then you put her in your pocket 'til next time.

STAN: Right.

RIP: So where was I?

STAN: Her place.

RIP: Billows of pillows. She was a natural redhead, know what I mean? Hundred percent Irish, believe me. She sparkled like Waterford crystal. I took out my dipstick to precheck. She was oozing with oil. We were in park at the head of the strip. I twisted her starter. We kicked over into a steady uphill climb in low. I fit like she was custom-made. When the rhythm was right, I threw her into first. We took off like two T-birds dragging down a dirt road. Pumping pistons. Supercharged eight-cylinder. Threw it into second. She was in spasms. Forced it into third. She blew my circuit. I flipped her over into reverse. We smoked. One greased engine. All jets blasting. To the bone. Busting the sound barrier. To the wire. My face pressurized into contortions. Two gees, five gees, nine gees. We began fishtailing. Her hips double-jointed. A spiritual experience. The Ascension. The Second Coming. Flailing tongues of fire. A litany to

Act One

the saints. The finish line. The flag went down. First place. I grabbed the trophy!

STAN: Wow.

RIP: (*Calming*) Afterward I cooled my jets. Tried to regulate my breath. She purred in idle. She even smelt like burnt rubber. I rolled onto the floor. She was stuttering and mumbling, trying to form the words 'thank you', but her lips were too spent. Like an angel, she came down to Earth wrapped in swirling clouds of sheets. I said, 'Hey baby, you deserved it.' And disappeared.

STAN: What was her name?

RIP: Her name? Who cares what her name was? (*Boastingly*) But I bet she remembers my name 'til she dies. Rip. 'Cause I ripped her to pieces. Aces.

STAN: Spades. (*He pours* RIP *a cup of coffee.*)

RIP: What'd you do last night? Pull pud?

STAN: (*Defensively*) That's not funny.

RIP: Slam ham?

STAN: I don't like that, Rip.

RIP: Beat meat? Meter your peter? Choke the chicken? Just joshing.

STAN: Yeah, right.

RIP: Hey, Stan, good cup o' mud.

STAN: Yeah.

RIP: (*Trying to cheer* STAN.) Really 'Mountain Grown'.

STAN: (*Seriously*) Got it on sale. Got a good deal on toilet paper, too. Coupons.

RIP: Doing your job. Thatta boy. You clean the tub drain?

STAN: Just like you said. Rotorooter.

RIP: Good boy.

STAN: Bowling.

RIP: Coupons on bowling?

STAN: Last night. That's what I did.

RIP: You alone?

STAN: Myself.

RIP: Gotta get a chick, Stan. A polished bumper.

STAN: I dunno.

RIP: You don't know. Where's my bagel? (STAN *gives him the bagel. He bites into it. Repulsion skids across his face. Angrily.*) How many times do I tell you, Stan? How many times? Go to Joey. Walk right back to the cook station. Don't deal with Tits Malone at the counter and ask Joey for a smear. He always does me good. But you gotta tell him the bagel's for me.

STAN: Joey's day off.

RIP: Joey's day off. Then Tony. Tony.

STAN: Tony gave me that.

RIP: You told him it was me?

STAN: I said you were the bagel.

(*Pause*)

RIP: Fucking Tony. Fucking burnt-bagel, no-smear Tony. This is a dry piece of ash. Last time. Joey's not there, you don't go in. You hear me?

STAN: I hear.

RIP: You walk in, it's Joey's day off, you don't even look at Tony. You spin your wheels and speed right outta that greasehole. Watch it you don't slide back in on the way out. Hairpit. (*Pause. Sincerely.*) Hey, Stan. (*Pause*) You want this?

ACT ONE

STAN: No thanks.

RIP: Here. Take it. You never eat no more. That's not good you don't eat. C'mon. Take it.

STAN: No, really. I'm never hungry.

(RIP *flips the bagel to* STAN.)

RIP: Then throw that hockey puck in the garbage. (STAN *shoots the bagel into the wastepaper basket.*) Swish! Two points. (*Matter-of-factly*) You can start on that toaster there. One side of the bread doesn't toast. One of the heating element units must be busted. The nichrome wire. I don't know which one. Get a solderless spade for a number sixteen wire.

STAN: Okay.

(*To fix the toaster,* STAN *needs a pair of long-nose pliers and a terminal connector: a small piece of bendable tin. All work is done inside the toaster, so nothing is visible. After testing the toaster to see which wire is out, he puts the connector over the inner wires and bends it with the pliers to conform and hold tight.*)

RIP: So on the way to the shop, I bump into the two natives from the island of Lesbos.

STAN: Greta and Bonnie?

RIP: They were holding hands. Disgusting. I don't understand it. Two foxy chicks. (*Pause. Emphatically.*) I want them. Both together. One alone. I don't care. (*Pause*) I told them the only reason they're gay is that they haven't gotten a taste of the Master Mojo himself. The Washington Monument.

STAN: So what'd they say?

RIP: They tried to slice me with their usual dyke rhetoric, pointing me out as a prime example of low-life male buffoonery. How ridiculous. So I say, 'Come on now, Gret-babe, tell the truth. Which is really stronger? The tongue or the sword?'

STAN: You said that?

RIP: Did I say I said that? I said that. (*Noticing* STAN *with the pliers in the toaster.*) Watch it pressing those wires. Easy.

STAN: Gotcha. (*He presses easily and pulls out the pliers.*)

RIP: Solid. Pretty soon you'll be fixing more than simple appliances, Stan.

STAN: I want to repair radios next.

RIP: In time.

STAN: I think I can do it now.

RIP: You will. But first you gotta drill the basics.

STAN: I know the basics.

RIP: You know nothing.

STAN: What about the treat machine?

RIP: What about it?

STAN: Can we work on it?

RIP: We just kicked over the engine, we're not even out of the parking lot of this day.

STAN: Aw, c'mon, Rip. The treat machine.

RIP: I don't want to hear about it 'til later. Work. Then treat.

STAN: Work the machine just a little now.

RIP: Not during working hours. Stall, Stan. (STAN *is noticeably disappointed and falls silent.*) Now drill. Electric is a Greek word meaning—

STAN: Amber.

RIP: Electric force means—

STAN: The force of attraction and repulsion.

Rip: How much do we know about electricity more than the ancient Greeks?

Stan: Nothing. We know the laws of electricity and use them. But we still don't know what electricity actually is.

Rip: Aces. Saying an engine is the force that moves an automobile is describing the effect, not the force itself.

Stan: (*Monotonously*) The force of electricity is a mystery. (*Impatiently*) I know all this. You sledgehammer me daily with this stuff!

Rip: I know you know.

Stan: I know you know I know.

Rip: I know. Tread my track, Stan. You'll be able to hold a busted radio in your hand and feel what's wrong. Instinctively. By taking in the whole, you'll know the specific. But now you must learn the specifics to grasp a sense of the whole. An electrician is more than knowing the theory of electricity and a use of tools. It's a whole perception of life. A mechanic has more than a job. He's got a logical thought process to adapt reality. Hear what I just said? Adaptability. Man must adapt. What living things thrive equal to Man? Insects. Why? Adaptability. They genetically adapt to the environment. Man physically adapts the environment to himself. We change the outside. Insects change the inside. If we could learn to adapt genetically, we'd be one up on the bugs. Adaptability.

Stan: Adaptability.

Rip: Man must adapt to survive. Sometimes to survive himself. (*Pause*) Stan, life is adapting 'til death. (*Pause*) I know you're lost. I'll do you a favor and show you something you're not ready for. What better way to adapt life than with an adaptor. Literally. I control electricity. Alter life through the systems I create. My own rules. Transform energy. Change matters. Adapt eveything to my own circuit. (*He pulls out a blueprint.*) This is a custom-made blueprint of an electronic stereo system for Mr. Big Bucks. Only the rich can afford simplicity. This joker doesn't lift a finger. All he has to do is get out of bed. The system does the rest. His feet hit a panel that switches off the alarm and turns on a pre-chosen tape. When he leaves the bedroom, an electronic eye-beam across the doorway tricks off and tranfers the music into the next room. And then into the next room and so on. The music follows him wherever he goes. There are selector switches placed throughout the house if he wants to alter the program at any time. When he leaves, the front door shuts off the system. Smooth as satin on silk, right? During the day, if he gets into an unexpected mood, like his chick tells him to screw off, he phones home, the system picks up his call, he punches in a song so when he walks in the front door it's playing 'Breaking Up Is Hard To Do' or whatever. Now there's one slight problem. I'm doing his kitchen, too. He can actually call up and cook dinner over the phone. But there's a limited amount of circuits in the actual telephone, so he has to go through two steps. I'd like to get it down to one. (*Pause. Sincerely.*) Maybe you can help me with that one day, Stan. Anyway, this is just the stereo system; a Jew's harp compared to the symphony in the kitchen.

STAN: (*Genuinely impressed.*) Wow.

RIP: That's what you can do if you stick with me, kid. But meanwhile, test that bin of batteries.

(STAN *looks out the window and unconsciously imitates* RIP's *manner of speaking.*)

STAN: Look at that bumper!

RIP: Where?

STAN: Next to the fire hydrant. Take a shine to those headlights.

Act One

Rip: Low idle. She's an antique.

Stan: Like to shift her into four-wheel drive.

Rip: Junk her.

Stan: Got character. The home feel.

Rip: Rusty.

Stan: Nice eyes.

Rip: Shift yours and fetch a needle-nose pliers.

Stan: I think I forgot.

Rip: You remember you forgot where you stashed it two minutes ago?

Stan: Yeah.

Rip: Scour for it.

Stan: (*Looking back out the window.*) Right.

Rip: Bow wow bit the breeze.

Stan: Check.

Rip: Where'd you put it?

Stan: Away.

Rip: (*Pointing*) Catch that action.

Stan: On the tool rack?

Rip: Yeah.

Stan: (*Giggling nervously*) Never put it where it's supposed to be. Threw me.

(Rip *picks up the newspaper and crosses to the washroom.*)

Rip: My gut's gunning the juice. Gotta dump your mud. Put the batteries through paces.

Stan: Solid.

(Rip *exits.* Stan *takes some batteries out of the bin and places them on the worktable. He picks one up and slowly comes to a freeze. He stands motionless, his eyes vacant, for a silent period of time. Suddenly,* RIP *shouts from the washroom.*)

RIP: Genetics, Stan!

STAN: (*Softly*) Genetics.

RIP: What were we talking about?

STAN: Bumpers.

RIP: Adaptability. Right here in the daily. Nuclear testing in the Fifties. Those soldiers' genes are scrambled, now. The ones who saw the explosions. Diseased. Altered. Just the jam I was jawing. Genetic disaster. (*He flushes the toilet.* STAN *snaps from his pose and dumps the untested batteries into a bin.* RIP *enters.*) Finish testing those batteries?

STAN: Yeah.

RIP: Good boy. Take apart that iron. The steam doesn't shoot.

STAN: Routine.

(STAN *places the iron on the worktable, plugs it in and gets tools.*)

RIP: Ditto. Physical disease isn't the only thing passed through genes. Emotional distress. You listening?

STAN: (*Distantly*) Emotional distress.

RIP: Emotional dysfunction. I'm not talking to the wall.

(RIP *pushes him verbally.* STAN *barely fends him off.*)

STAN: Can we work on the treat machine?

RIP: Behavior related to chemical constitution.

STAN: Yeah.

RIP: Do you read?

STAN: Loud and clear.

Act One

RIP: Passed blood.

STAN: Over and out.

RIP: Catch the drift?

STAN: Snowbound.

RIP: Adaptable disease.

STAN: Check.

RIP: Compute?

STAN: Registered.

RIP: Inheritance.

STAN: Ease off the gas pedal.

RIP: Adam raising Cain.

(STAN *burns his hand on the iron.*)

STAN: Fuck! The fucking thing's fucked! Fuck it!

(*Silence.*)

RIP: (*Quietly*) Ice is in the fridge. (*He unplugs the iron. STAN gets the ice and holds it on his burn. Simply.*) You don't plug in an appliance to work on it. (*Pause*) Back to basics.

STAN: I can't.

RIP: It's necessary. Help you buck the burn. Transformer.

STAN: A device that changes energy potential from one circuit to another.

RIP: D.C.

STAN: Direct current.

RIP: Me to you. A.C.

STAN: Alternate current.

RIP: Our dyke friends. AC/DC.

STAN: Two-way current.

RIP: Tell her to bring her girlfriend. (*Pause*) Battery.

STAN: Two or more cells placed in a common container. One dominant.

RIP: Let me eyeball your burn. (*He looks at* STAN's *hand.*) It's nothing. Y'know, we're like a battery on a baseball team. I'm pitching and you're catching.

STAN: And I'm the one who gets hit in the balls.

(BRANDY *enters. She moves and dresses seductively, and speaks with a Kentucky accent. Confident in her sexual appeal, she tries to fit into* RIP's *image of a woman. Teasing and flirting, she plays into his hand. She wears at least one article of clothing that is red.*)

BRANDY: Any bull ready to charge red?

RIP: There's my spark plug. That transmitter of passion waves. My machine called woman.

BRANDY: I wanna suck on a pop so I came. (STAN *goes to the refrigerator.*) Mountain Dew.

RIP: Attack your mechanic panic.

(BRANDY *jumps onto* RIP, *wrapping her legs around his waist.*)

BRANDY: I'll hop on your horn anytime.

RIP: (*Proclaiming*) Brandy: a drink that boils the blood. Sweet, but with a kick.

BRANDY: I love when you say that.

RIP: You love when anyone says that.

BRANDY: I do not.

RIP: You do too.

BRANDY: Don't.

RIP: Do.

ACT ONE 15

BRANDY: Don't.

RIP: Stan, you say it.

STAN: (*Holding a soda.*) We don't have Mountain Dew today. Coke.

BRANDY: Fine. (*She slides off* RIP *and takes the soda.*)

RIP: Say it.

STAN: Say what?

BRANDY: Say what my name means.

STAN: Brandy's a drink.

BRANDY: Go on.

STAN: Maybe an aperitif.

RIP: Stan, she wants you to say it like me to see if it gets the juices going.

BRANDY: Shut up, crude thing!

STAN: Oh. . . . You drink it to get drunk and it kicks you.

BRANDY: (*Taking a step toward* STAN *seductively.*) And it's sweet.

STAN: Sweet.

BRANDY: (*Considering the effect, then decisively.*) See! Nothing! (*Hugging* RIP.) It's you, you, you!

RIP: So what? No chick gets hot over anything Stan says. What's that prove? I'm saying if it's past the shank of night, you're alone, and you've dumped a few belts down your throat, any member of the male species, provided his face don't look like he's been kissing cars on the highway, sashays up to you and kicks out that same line, you fall into orgasm chasm.

BRANDY: You couldn't be more wrong, but I love when my man's jealous. Give mamma some sugar. (*They kiss.*) Hey. Where were you last night?

RIP: Uhh—

BRANDY: I was tapping my toes all night at Jimmy's Bar. Got sloshed waiting on you.

RIP: Went bowling with Stan.

BRANDY: Bowling. Like with balls?

STAN: Yep, Rip kept balling the same angel all night long.

BRANDY: Angel?

RIP: Bowling slang, Brandy.

STAN: Kept knocking down the same pin over and over again.

RIP: (*To* STAN) Stall.

BRANDY: Thought you were supposed to knock 'em all down.

STAN: He's trying but he was having a hard time with only one last night.

RIP: Kill the engine.

BRANDY: Why didn't you come and pick me up at the bar?

STAN: When we gonna work on the treat machine?

RIP: Not now, Stan.

BRANDY: You said you'd meet me there.

STAN: During lunch break?

BRANDY: Why couldn't I go, too?

RIP: It was just guys, you'd 'a' been bored.

BRANDY: No I wouldn't 'a'.

STAN: The treat machine.

RIP: Boys' night out.

STAN: The machine.

RIP: Sweep it under the rug.

BRANDY: What's a treat machine?

RIP: You done with that iron yet?

STAN: It's done the iron. Now the treat.

BRANDY: What's he talking about?

RIP: Nothing. Something we're working on in our spare time.

BRANDY: Oh.

STAN: We gonna work it today?

RIP: Maybe. Zip it up for now.

STAN: When today?

RIP: (*Annoyed*) Stan! Put it in neutral.

BRANDY: He's really rattling on. I know something that'll take his mind off it. From one machine to another. Sinks the mind of any man. Takes an elevator to the middle floor. (*She approaches* STAN *slowly.*)

RIP: Oh, Jeez. Constipate, Stan. Take a sip of Brandy. But let me warn you, don't pop your clutch too soon. Advice from a driver with a winning track record.

BRANDY: Oh, Rip.

RIP: And watch it. A blown rod can crack your block.

(STAN *backs away from* BRANDY, *embarrassed and hurt.*)

STAN: Gotta go to the john.

RIP: Hey, you didn't constipate him.

(RIP *and* BRANDY *laugh.* STAN *exits to the washroom.*)

BRANDY: He's funny. Jealous?

RIP: You kidding? Stan's a hard charge. We're buddies. (*Seriously warning.*) But I see you with some

Neanderthal whistling a goon tune, I write a surprise ending to the same story. Know what I mean? I see you even talking to the pig patrol at the gas station down the alley, for instance, you even turn your head toward them, and there's fists flying. Those dupes stick their pumps into rear fenders all day. It goes to their brains, believe me. They pump ethyl. Mary. Judy. Anything with a motor. But Stan, I could never get jealous of Stan. Our wires weave within the same insulation.

BRANDY: He's weird. Never says a word. Spooky. He's like one of the busted appliances in this shop.

RIP: He's stalled. Just needs a jump.

BRANDY: You use him like a tool around here. I get that. But why buddy-buddy? You go bowling with him. Why not me? You didn't even tell me.

RIP: I did tell you.

BRANDY: Too late.

RIP: Better late than never.

BRANDY: I didn't even know you liked bowling. You don't tell me nothing. I don't even know whether to believe you. Oh, I don't know, Rip.

RIP: You don't know what Rip?

BRANDY: I don't know what I don't know.

RIP: Then what are you saying?

BRANDY: I guess I'm saying that I don't know if I can believe you all the time.

RIP: You don't trust me?

BRANDY: Yes I do, but—

RIP: I'm a liar.

BRANDY: No, I don't mean that. It's just . . . well. . . . You think I'm some kinda dummy. Like I don't see you. Like I just accept what you say. Do what you say.

RIP: You do do what I say.

BRANDY: Where were you last night?

RIP: How much of a lunch break can you steal?

BRANDY: What d'ya mean?

RIP: I'm gonna pop your hubcaps and rip the leather off your seat.

BRANDY: I'm talking last night.

RIP: I'm talking now. I'm talking flush what you *think* happened out of your system. Talking about the hard facts in private.

BRANDY: Oh, Rip, I don't know. I'm dizzy. A lotta men want me, y'know.

RIP: I know. And you know what?

BRANDY: What?

RIP: I'll knock them down and tiptoe on their faces. Let's blow this popstand. (*Pause*) I want only you.

BRANDY: You do?

RIP: You.

BRANDY: Me?

RIP: You.

BRANDY: Really?

RIP: Only you.

BRANDY: Sure?

RIP: You.

BRANDY: Rip.

(*They kiss.*)

RIP: Let's blow the circuit breaker.

BRANDY: Oh, hon.

RIP: (*Shouting to* STAN.) I'm taking an early lunch. You know what to work. Lamps. And especially the car battery. Recharge.

BRANDY: Your place or mine?

RIP: Flip for it.

BRANDY: Heads or tails?

RIP: Head at your place, tail at mine.

BRANDY: Rip! (*To* STAN) You can come out now, we're leaving!

RIP: Can it, let's buzz.

(*They exit.* STAN *enters. He takes a battery out of the bin, flips it into the air, and catches it. He does this again. And again. He throws the battery viciously against the wall, runs in the opposite direction and smashes his hand into the wall.* STAN *collapses onto the floor, curling into a fetal position.*)

BLACKOUT

Scene 2

(*Midafternoon of the same day.* RIP *and* STAN *are working.* STAN *repairs a lamp. His sprained hand is wrapped in an ace bandage. He is deeply depressed to the point of agitation and paranoid misinterpretation.*)

RIP: How's the lamp coming?

STAN: Fine.

RIP: Put your finger on the short?

STAN: 'Course not. I'm no dummy. Don't like getting shocked.

RIP: I meant did you locate the problem?

Act One

Stan: Oh. Yeah.

Rip: Switch?

Stan: To what?

Rip: The problem.

Stan: I don't have a problem.

Rip: Who said you did?

Stan: You did.

Rip: I did.

Stan: You.

Rip: Me.

Stan: Yeah.

Rip: When?

Stan: Just now.

Rip: Okay. (*Pause*) Wire?

Stan: No, I'm not. I'm fine.

Rip: I know you're fine.

Stan: Leave me alone.

Rip: All I'm asking is what's the problem. Where's the short in the lamp? The switch or the wire?

(*Pause*)

Stan: Oh. Switch.

(*Pause*)

Rip: Thank God we got that settled. A little small talk. Loosen up. Relax. (*Chanting*) Stan! Stan! He's our man! If he can't do it nobody can! Hey, hey, hey. My main man, Stan. Recharge. You look android. (*He puts up his fists.*) Okay. I'm Mohammed Ali and you're Cassius Clay.

Stan: Which fight?

RIP: Dukes up and we'll see which fight. (*He prances around* STAN *in a boxing stance. They duck and weave.*) Your behind will be mine in nine! You'll take a dive in five no jive! (STAN *lets his hands fall to his sides.*) You're boxing like Sonny Listless. (*He clips* STAN *with three quick, open-hand slaps in the face.*) Wake up.

STAN: Dont' feel like it.

RIP: You don't feel like it.

STAN: Right.

RIP: Right. (*Pause*) What do you feel like?

STAN: Nothing.

RIP: Not even the treat machine?

STAN: The treat machine?

RIP: Did I say the treat machine? The machine.

STAN: Work on it now?

RIP: Am I asking you now?

STAN: Yeah.

RIP: Then now.

STAN: During working hours?

RIP: Uh-oh. Are these working hours?

STAN: (*Disappointedly*) Yeah.

RIP: I'll get it.

STAN: Wow!

(BRANDY *enters.*)

BRANDY: Shucks, sugar! Rock and roll me! Cut me a mean rug! Buck and wing me daddy to the blare of brass!

RIP: You were put on this planet to satisfy earthly desires.

Act One 23

Brandy: I swoon to your tune.

Rip: To clean my points.

Brandy: And I got big news.

Stan: We gonna work on this thing?

Brandy: I'm serious.

Rip: We're ears.

Brandy: It's a—

Stan: Should I get it?

Brandy: Tell him to shut up. I zip my lip and you lose a gold mine.

Rip: Money?

Brandy: Jonathan Whitehall saw the system you created for Mr. Bush and he wants an original system designed by you for his kitchen. His wife's a gourmet cook. And his money's contagious. Does that goose your gong?

Rip: I got gadgets spilling out of my head! I'm taking this guy to the cleaners! Like taking Fort Knox from a baby. Mint condition sucker. (*Pause*) Foot the clutch. How do you know this?

Brandy: He's a friend of my boss. He told me 'cause he thought I'd get a commission from you or something.

Rip: More like something. Your commission is me letting you work overtime in the sack. (*Abruptly leaving her and going to* Stan.) You paying attention? This is what I'm talking about. Adaptability.

Stan: Adaptability.

Rip: I adapt electricity to invent gizmos. I adapt moneybags to give me cash for those gizmos. Adaptability. Love it.

Brandy: (*Not thrilled*) He wants you there at one.

RIP: It's twenty-to now.

BRANDY: Here's the address. (*She holds out a slip of paper.* RIP *reaches for it. She pulls the number away from him.*) How about a little thank you at least. Ain't gonna hurt you none.

RIP: No more mouthing. Gotta go. (*Pause*) Alright. C'mere baby. (*She approaches him. He gives her a quick peck on the cheek and grabs the note from her.*) Thank you, darlin'.

BRANDY: You louse.

STAN: The thing.

RIP: Later. Business is business, right?

STAN: But . . . yeah. (*He exits into the washroom.*)

BRANDY: What thing?

RIP: No thing. But listen. You stay here with Stan.

BRANDY: What?

RIP: Hard of hearing? Read my lips. Stay. Here. With. Stan.

BRANDY: Why?

RIP: Because.

BRANDY: Because why?

RIP: Because I say so.

BRANDY: I don't want to.

RIP: Why?

BRANDY: Because.

RIP: Because why?

BRANDY: Because because.

RIP: Answer the damn question.

BRANDY: Because I want to be with you.

RIP: You want fireworks, blown cannons and general sexual warfare tonight, you plant your butt here and keep an eye on him.

BRANDY: Why does he have to be watched?

RIP: Say you'll do it.

BRANDY: Not 'til you give me a good reason.

RIP: Alright, alright, alright. Level. Look in my eyes. He hurt his hand this morning. He's in fragile condition. I want someone with him.

BRANDY: Baby got a boo-boo. Big deal. I stopped babysitting when I was fourteen.

RIP: Okay. You're forcing me.

BRANDY: Into what?

RIP: Do you love me?

BRANDY: Oh, come on, Rip.

RIP: Do you love me?

BRANDY: Please.

RIP: Do you love me?

BRANDY: You know I do.

RIP: Really love me?

BRANDY: Yes.

RIP: If you love me you'll stay with Stan.

BRANDY: You rat.

RIP: Back in a flash when the deal's a meal. (*Loudly*) See ya, Stan.

BRANDY: Good luck.

RIP: Aces. (*He exits.*)

BRANDY: Spades.

(STAN *enters. Unaware of her presence, he eats aspirin from the bottle. He turns and sees her. They both jump.*)

STAN: Oh.

BRANDY: Oh.

STAN: (*Simultaneously with* BRANDY.) I didn't know you were here.

BRANDY: (*Simultaneously with* STAN.) I didn't know you didn't know I was here.

(*Pause*)

STAN: (*Putting the bottle into his pocket.*) Why?

BRANDY: What?

STAN: What do you mean what?

BRANDY: I mean what do you mean why.

STAN: Why . . . why?

BRANDY: Why what?

STAN: Why are you here?

BRANDY: Oh. Uh . . . well . . . 'cause I didn't want to go with Rip.

STAN: Why?

BRANDY: 'Cause I thought I'd interfere.

STAN: Oh. Why are you here?

BRANDY: You already asked me that.

STAN: You already didn't answer it.

BRANDY: Well, just pretend I'm not here.

STAN: You are.

BRANDY: I am.

STAN: I am.

BRANDY: You are.

STAN: Why?

BRANDY: Why what?

STAN: Why do you want me to pretend you're not here?

BRANDY: Why not?

STAN: Why?

BRANDY: Because I don't want to interfere.

STAN: You don't want to interfere with Rip so you're *not* with him. You don't want to interfere with me so you *are* with me.

BRANDY: Alright. Why I'm really here is that, well, we see each other every day but we don't really talk, so I thought maybe this would be a good chance to get to know each other better.

(*Pause*)

STAN: Wanna coke?

BRANDY: I'd love one, thanks.

STAN: In the fridge.

BRANDY: Oh, sure. (*Going to the refrigerator.*) You?

STAN: No.

BRANDY: (*Opening the soda.*) So. (STAN *begins to work.*) So. (*Silence*) So you don't talk much, do you?

STAN: No.

BRANDY: Didn't think so. See, I knew that about you. That's one thing I did know.

STAN: Yeah.

BRANDY: Got a headache?

STAN: Why?

BRANDY: Saw you take some aspirin.

STAN: Always.

BRANDY: Headaches?

STAN: So aspirin.

BRANDY: Ah. See, I didn't know that about you. Not that.

STAN: Yeah.

(*Pause*)

BRANDY: I don't get headaches.

STAN: No.

BRANDY: Just hangover headaches. Nothing a shot of Tabasco in tomato juice can't cure. And a black cup of coffee. Maybe a green and red pepper omelet with cheese.

STAN: Yeah.

BRANDY: Headaches. Yeah, see, I didn't know that. That's interesting.

STAN: Yeah.

(*Pause*)

BRANDY: Bet you're like me, get 'em mostly in the morning.

STAN: All day.

BRANDY: That's what I thought.

STAN: I'm not like you.

BRANDY: That's what I thought. (*Pause*) Must be hard to concentrate with headaches all the time.

STAN: Hard to think.

BRANDY: Must be.

STAN: Thinking's the problem.

(*Silence*)

BRANDY: What do you like to do? For fun?

STAN: I like to sit and think of nothing. Or watch T.V. Same thing.

BRANDY: Oh.

STAN: Have you ever pitched a penny into a wishing well?

BRANDY: Sure as heck have.

STAN: What do you wish?

BRANDY: I always wish for a big, handsome, strong man to rescue me from a tall tower and live happily ever after. All girls do.

STAN: Some man like Rip?

BRANDY: Well, sorta, I guess . . . What do you wish?

STAN: Well, when I toss the coin, once it hits the water, I lose it. I can only see myself in the ripples. I feel more like that broken reflection than either the person looking into the pond or the wish sinking to the bottom. I'm stuck on the surface, all busted up, caught somewhere between what I am and what I hope to be.

BRANDY: (*Uncomfortably*) Oh. (*Silence*) So. (*Pause*) So Rip. So Rip is something. So Rip is really something, isn't he?

STAN: Oh, yeah. I like Rip a lot.

BRANDY: I like Rip a lot, too. You're the devil's disciple, aren't you.

STAN: Teaches me everything.

BRANDY: He's taught me a few things, too. Secrets wild horses couldn't drag out of me.

STAN: He's a trickster, alright. Scarves up both sleeves.

BRANDY: A magician.

STAN: Doves in his top hat.

BRANDY: Houdini. He can escape any predicament. You handcuff him with a tuxedo and throw him into a river full of socialites, he'll get free. I betcha this very minute he's handling Whitehall with kid gloves. I've seen him seduce with a velvet tongue and bust heads at the same time.

STAN: He's a pal. He's a teacher, a protector—

BRANDY: A lover.

STAN: I don't know about that.

BRANDY: I bet you know in a way.

STAN: What are you saying?

BRANDY: He must tell you things he wouldn't tell me.

STAN: I don't know.

BRANDY: 'Course he does.

STAN: Maybe.

BRANDY: Sure he does.

STAN: Guess so.

BRANDY: You're his confidant.

STAN: I don't know.

BRANDY: Sure you are.

STAN: In a way.

BRANDY: You listen to him more than eight hours a day. You hear his lingo more than anyone.

STAN: Maybe.

BRANDY: Of course you do.

STAN: So, maybe so.

BRANDY: (*Strongly*) There's no so maybe in it. You do.

STAN: Alright.

ACT ONE

BRANDY: So maybe, you can tell me something about Rip from a male perspective, huh?

STAN: I don't know.

BRANDY: 'Course you could. Unless you don't love him.

STAN: I do love him.

BRANDY: I love him, too. And when you love someone, you want to know everything about that person.

STAN: Guess so.

BRANDY: 'Course so. If you really love him, you'll tell me. (*Pause*) Rip loves women, right?

STAN: In a way.

BRANDY: What do you mean in a way?

STAN: Like a monkey wrench.

(*Silence*)

BRANDY: What?

STAN: You adjust women to fit your nut. And you can't get through life without a good wrench.

BRANDY: I can't believe you just said that.

STAN: Rip said that.

BRANDY: You're a liar.

STAN: You said to tell you what he says.

BRANDY: I didn't ask you to lie.

STAN: You know it's the truth.

BRANDY: I don't.

STAN: You should.

BRANDY: That's you talking not Rip.

STAN: This is Rip talking through me.

BRANDY: (*Roughly*) You'd like to be Rip. You hang on his every word. You're empty begging to be filled with him. To be him. Shadow. Puppet. Parrot. (*Trying to control herself.*) Okay. Does Rip see other women?

(STAN *begins to walk, gesture, and speak like* RIP. *He takes a battery from the bin, flips it into the air and catches it.*)

STAN: You really want to get to know me better, baby?

BRANDY: I said I did and keep the babies to yourself.

STAN: Grease my engine.

BRANDY: You need more than grease to get your engine slick. Some punk poured sand in your fuel tank.

STAN: I got a jack of all trades in my trunk and brand spanking new rubber treads on tires bulging from my back can. Muscled reinforcements. Jack you up and spin your wheels.

BRANDY: You're a stalled Studebaker, son. A fresh lemon slipping sour from the factory track. A virgin fender bender. So jack, don't jack a load you can't handle.

STAN: (*Approaching her.*) Screw your bolts.

BRANDY: You wouldn't know how to strip my bolts, so don't pump your puny piston when it's only gonna melt soon as my engine heats up too hot.

STAN: (*Embracing her.*) Adjust your steering column. Rearrange your A-frame.

BRANDY: (*Slipping away from him.*) Can the corn, cornball.

STAN: Smash your windshield.

BRANDY: Honey, you're a big brute and I'm sure you're a dreamboat for some gal, who knows who, but your wheels are spinning in quicksand; you're sinking lower than I thought possible.

STAN: Strip your transmission.

BRANDY: You're a live socket, Stan, but throw the master switch to off, sweetie.

STAN: (*Touching her in a sexual way.*) Muffle your muffler.

BRANDY: (*Forcefully breaking away.*) Alright, listen. You're trying to act like Rip. I want the charade to stop right now.

STAN: (*Returning to himself. Accusingly.*) You're acting like Rip.

BRANDY: You live through Rip.

STAN: *You* live through Rip.

BRANDY: (*Viciously demeaning*) Alright, fuckhead! I tried to be nice. I tried, believe me. You think I'm here to get to know you better? C'mon queersome. Rip made me stay here. Why? Because you're a helpless, toothless baby without a bite. Why don't you live your own life? You suck on Rip like a pacifier. Leave me and Rip alone. Get out of our lives! You freak! You Frankenstein!

(STAN *smashes his fist savagely into her face. She flies backwards and collapses onto the floor. He kicks her in the ribs. She screams and loses consciousness. He is a frantic bundle of incomplete actions. He whimpers as if wounded. He slams his head onto the worktable and falls unconscious next to* BRANDY. RIP *enters.*)

RIP: We're having filet mignon as appetizers with this guy! He's a cinch. (*He sees the bodies. He goes to* STAN, *then* BRANDY, *then back to* STAN *again. He holds* STAN *in his arms and rocks him.*) Stan, Stan, Stan, I'm sorry. (*He goes to the telephone and dials.*) Send an ambulance immediately to 1601 Fullerton. At Ashland. Rip's Electric. A woman's had an accident.

Thank you. (*He drags* STAN *across the room as the lights fade.*)

BLACKOUT

Scene 3

(*Evening.* RIP *bandages* STAN'S *forehead.*)

RIP: Patch you up like a bicycle tire. Stop that leak. Take a sip. (STAN *takes a sip of soda.*) Thatta boy. Feel better?

STAN: A little. What time is it?

RIP: Almost dark. How's your headache?

STAN: Sparks between my temples.

RIP: Feel a hum?

STAN: Yeah. Why are your eyes like that?

RIP: Do you know where Brandy is?

STAN: At home?

RIP: No.

STAN: I don't know then.

RIP: Do you remember talking with Brandy after I left to go to Whitehall's?

STAN: Yeah. Why did she stay here?

RIP: I thought you only hurt yourself when you're alone. Do you remember blowing your top at Brandy?

STAN: No. I liked talking to her. (*Touching the bandage.*) Did I hurt myself? I remember talking and then I. . . . I don't know. You just woke me up, right?

RIP: Right.

STAN: Maybe I fell asleep. Why are your eyes like that? Did something bad happen?

Act One

Rip: I gotta tell you something, Stan. And I'm gonna give it to you straight. But first I wanna tell you something else. I love you.

Stan: I know.

Rip: I know you know.

Stan: I know you know I know.

Rip: I know. But I do. And I wanna say it anyway. You're closer than anything can get to me. We run on the same energy. Two prongs in the same plug. Together we're a working unit that's unstoppable. That's what I want to tell you before I tell you what I really gotta tell you.

Stan: I do you, too.

Rip: I know you do, too.

Stan: But what do you got to tell me?

Rip: What I gotta tell you is because I love you something's got to happen.

Stan: Happen.

Rip: Yeah.

Stan: Happen.

Rip: Yeah.

Stan: To what?

Rip: To who.

Stan: To who?

Rip: To who.

Stan: So who?

Rip: You.

Stan: To me?

Rip: Right.

STAN: To me.

RIP: To you.

STAN: Why?

(*Pause*)

RIP: Your body is a powerhouse of electricity. A complex, simple mass of raw power.

STAN: Thank you. I mean it.

RIP: But.

STAN: But what?

RIP: But your brain.

STAN: But my brain.

RIP: Your brain.

STAN: I know my brain. I was never good in school.

RIP: I'm not talking about school, I'm talking about real life. Your brain has gone through a type of assault. Battery. The system of your brain is supercharged but misdirected. A secondhand hand-down. But it's only genes, you can't help it. Like a slashed telephone wire spitting in a storm. The storm's natural. Couldn't be helped. But the wire must be repaired for communication to be restored. It's not your fault, so relax.

STAN: I'm not nervous.

RIP: Good you're not nervous. (*Pause*) It's time, Stan.

STAN: For what?

RIP: The treat machine.

STAN: To work on it?

RIP: For it to work on you.

STAN: Is it done?

RIP: Totally finished. Tested. Performs to precision.

ACT ONE

STAN: It's finished? It's time to do it?

RIP: Yes.

STAN: You said it'll calm me down. You said it'll change me. You said I could control myself. You said I won't hurt myself. You said—Can I get another coke?

RIP: Sure, Stan.

STAN: (*Getting a soda.*) You said—But it's ready now?

RIP: Yes. But sit down and listen to me like I'm your father.

STAN: Sure, Rip. Spit it out. (*He knocks over the soda.*) I'm sorry.

RIP: That's fine.

STAN: I'll wipe it up.

RIP: Now listen.

STAN: It's finished.

RIP: Put it in park. Sedate! (STAN *falls silent and still.*) The machine has been in perfect working order for the last few days. That's why we haven't been working on it. I've been waiting for the right time. We are beyond the correct time. The next step is already in motion. (*He unlocks a drawer and takes out the treat machine. The machine is a simple black metal box approximately six inches high and twelve inches in both length and width. He holds the machine while he speaks reverently.*) This is our wonder box. A mystery to Merlin. The miracle light that guides through the maze of the mind. The Papal blessing cleansing generations of congenital sin. Kills Cain from Adam. Makes fruitful the rotten seed of genetic inheritance. Cools the boiling blood passed through wild fathers. This is my gift to you. Through this gift, I live through you.

STAN: What does that mean? I feel like you're gonna give me Communion. Like I'm dying and you're giving me Extreme Unction.

RIP: Sort of. Part of you will die. Heave out the bad, breathe in the good. Rebirth. A new baptism. Reincarnate to a higher stratification. You'll wear my imprimatur.

STAN: You speak Greek. What *is* that?

RIP: Aces.

STAN: Spades.

RIP: This is an E.C.T. device. Electroconvulsive therapy. Shock treatment.

(*Silence*)

STAN: I get enough shocks on the appliances, they do nothing for me.

RIP: What are the two most vital parts of the human body?

STAN: The brain and . . . uh . . . hands.

RIP: The brain and the heart.

STAN: The heart.

RIP: The heart is the pump. The timer. The regulator.

STAN: A gas pump in a car engine.

RIP: Right. The brain is the computer system which puts the body into action. The heart is like the common worker and the brain is like management. You're all heart, Stan.

STAN: And you're all brain?

RIP: That's beside the point. The heart and the brain must ride in stride to be a full-working mechanism. Like us. Like any electrical circuit. You're a manic-depressive, Stan.

Act One

STAN: I am?

RIP: You have high highs and low lows.

STAN: Manic-depressive.

RIP: When you're high, your speech and activity quicken. Your world is perceived like a sped-up movie. But frantic. Charlie Chaplin on fast forward. I think you were manic with Brandy. Depression is the opposite. Inactivity. You feel like you're worth a bucket of bent nails. Despair.

STAN: In my room, I look at the clock and realize I've been sitting there doing absolutely nothing for three hours. I lose track.

RIP: See? (*Pause*) This is a very simple machine. A high-school punk can assemble one. Sixteen-year-old kids have made small H-bombs for Chrissake. I could've built it blindfolded but I had you work on it with me so you feel it's a part of you.

STAN: The machine's not a stranger. I don't know the purpose of it but I always felt I was building a savior.

RIP: It is a savior. You're on to me! Yahweh to the genetically, emotionally disturbed. Genetics, Stan. You with me?

STAN: Yeah.

RIP: ECT is given in only genetic cases. Never given to people when the depression is caused by something that happens in your life. Never a disappointment caused by an event. The cause must be genetic. The blood of the family. An inherited disturbance. Until ECT, genetic insanity was considered incurable. The electrical stimulation gives control over the emotions. Electricity, Stan. The life force.

STAN: That night. That one night. I was twelve years old. Just me and my Ma living in the house. My Ma came to tuck me in. She hugged me but looked at me funny. My Ma, she giggled. A gurgle that started at the back of her throat like a baby playing with its own spit. Spitting up dribble. A giggle and a dribble. She smiled. Then looked angry. Then sighed. Relieved. Her eyes narrowed but she looked through me. Through my eyes. Through the back of my head, through the wallpaper and the brick of the building. And with that pin-point laser-look, she said, 'Go to sleep, son, but always dream to the limit, and your mind will travel beyond limits you have never dreamed.' Last thing she said to me. When I was little, Ma had bad moods, but only once in a while. She'd hug me afterward. I thought all moms were like that. A bad day. But she became worse and worse until she only had isolated moments of control. When she killed herself, I believe it was in one heroic moment of sanity.

(*Silence*)

RIP: I refuse to let you be a hero, Stan. No red badges of courage. You're gonna win this war by push-button electrics, not hand-to-hand combat on yourself.

STAN: But how do you know all this stuff? Genetics? ECT?

RIP: You don't trust me?

STAN: I just want to know.

RIP: Do you trust me?

STAN: Yeah, but—

RIP: Do you trust me?

STAN: You know I do.

RIP: Really trust me?

STAN: Yes.

RIP: If you trust me, don't ask.

STAN: I don't have to know.

(*Pause*)

RIP: I know you're curious, so I'm gonna tell you anyway.

STAN: Thanks, Rip.

RIP: You've been with me for a year.

STAN: About.

RIP: I've seen you get drastically worse.

STAN: Like my Ma?

RIP: Your memory is shot. You burned yourself on an iron, for Chrissake. When I saw you getting worse, I began to read. I ate books, Stan. I've spoken to clinical psychologists. I've visited clinics. I've seen patients. That's how I know what I'm doing, Stan.

STAN: (*With a sudden surge of fear.*) I'm scared. All those movies about busted arms and legs. Shaved heads. Naked bodies. Strapped and screaming faces. Coming out shock-rocked in the brain box. Like robots. Mean nurses and Nazi doctors. That's why I've never gone to those mental health centers. Scares the shit out of me.

RIP: I know, Stan. I know. I understand. And I'm going to respond to that in two words. Are you listening?

STAN: Yeah.

RIP: Bull. Shit. (*Silence*) Lies. Nothing to do with serious science. You know electricity is not to be feared, but to be—

STAN: Adapted.

RIP: Controlled.

STAN: Used.

RIP: A miracle! (*Pause*) Electric therapy with respect. ECT is not worse than the monster life you're living. Convulsive therapy saves some people more than God. (*Pause*) There is no personality change. (*Pause*) Most people undergoing treatment are out-patients. Most go back to work. Within an hour after the treatment the patient goes home. I spoke to one woman, pretty foxy chick actually, and she said she couldn't wait 'til her next treatment. That it literally saved her life. She didn't tell her boss about the treatment, took vacation time, and when she came back, the people in the office couldn't get over her positive attitude and control. She was fun to be with. Before ECT no one wanted to deal with her because she was too spooky. You with me, Stan?

STAN: Yeah, I'm here.

RIP: It has to happen.

STAN: I know.

RIP: Give me the green light.

STAN: Okay.

RIP: Let me hear it.

STAN: I do.

RIP: I do what? I don't want you to kick your own bucket.

STAN: I want the treat machine. I want to undergo ECT. With you at the board.

RIP: (*Hugging* STAN.) Thatta boy! I want to loose your noose. No one handles electricity like I do. The master adaptor. Remember I sucked you into a medical check-up?

STAN: Yeah. You said it was a union thing.

RIP: It was for this. You're refusing to eat, have insomnia and you're self-destructive. But you're in perfect physical shape to undergo treatment without a risk.

STAN: Thank you. I mean it.

RIP: Now I think you should hit the head. (*Pointing*) That head. (STAN *exits into the washroom.* RIP *takes out a medical bag and places it on the worktable. He takes out electrodes and plugs them into the machine.*

Act One

He plugs the machine cord into a live socket. STAN *enters.*) There's no pain because you'll be asleep. Sit here. (STAN *sits on the worktable. Using a small cloth,* RIP *cleans* STAN's *scalp and temples with a detergent. He rinses, dries, and rubs on an ointment. He places the electrodes on his head. To himself.*) I'll execute the bolus method with fixed amounts of anesthetic agents. Seventy milligrams of methoherital and one-hundred milligrams of succinylcholine. (*To* STAN.) I was drilled in the procedure by this gorgeous nurse I met at Buddy's Bar, so I know what I'm doing. I shot her with more than a needle, lemme tell ya. She helped me get the drugs, too. Everyone has a price, you better believe it. When the treatment begins, you'll experience a slight stimulation. It only involves a couple of muscles. The *seizure* relieves depression, not the shock. After the seizure, you'll be confused for about ten minutes. How you feeling?

STAN: Good as I can, knowing I'm going to get I don't know how many volts through my brain in a second.

RIP: Hundred and forty.

STAN: Thanks.

RIP: Much of the current is dissipated through the skull. Only small amounts reach the brain. Hug this treatment like a Pentecostalist hugs the Bible. Ready?

STAN: Ready.

RIP: All engines blast.

STAN: Recharge.

RIP: Aces.

STAN: Spades. (RIP *takes out two prefilled syringes.*) Can I get addicted to this?

RIP: (*Giving him one shot in the arm.*) Start counting backwards.

STAN: (*His speech becoming progressively more slurred.*) Ten, nine, eight, seven, six, hey, Rip.

RIP: Yeah.

STAN: One question.

RIP: Shoot. (*He shoots* STAN *with the second syringe.*)

STAN: Why are you doing this? Why don't I just go in to a clinic?

(STAN *loses consciousness. His mouth drops open.* STAN *falls gently into* RIP's *arms.* RIP *moves* STAN's *jaw up and down. It is flaccid. He lays* STAN *on his back onto the worktable.*)

RIP: I never take anything in. I always fix it myself.

(RIP *turns on the machine by simply pressing a button.* STAN's *body moves only slightly. His feet stretch and scarcely twitch. His head turns slowly to one side. Nothing more.*)

BLACKOUT

End of Act One

Act Two

Scene 1

(*The next day.* STAN *is prepared for another shock treatment.* RIP *shoots him with the first syringe.* BRANDY *knocks at the door.* RIP *is surprised.*)

BRANDY: (*Offstage*) Rip?

RIP: Just a minute.

BRANDY: Why's this door locked? (STAN *is nearly unconscious from the drug.* RIP *leads him into the washroom and leaves him in there.* RIP *unlocks the front door.* BRANDY *enters. An ugly bruise on her cheekbone dominates her face.*) I'm back, you hunk.

RIP: Hey, baby, what's rattling? (*He hugs her.*)

BRANDY: Owww! A couple of ribs.

RIP: Poor babe. (*He kisses her.*) You're out so soon. Didn't expect you. Was gonna pick you up.

BRANDY: I know you were, sweetie, but they discharged me early, thank God. (RIP *holds her in a hug, trying to keep her away from the washroom.*) Hold your horses, sugar, I gots to take a powder. Been hopping here with my legs crossed. (*She tries to pull out of his grip.* STAN *spills out of the washroom.*) What's he doing here?

RIP: He's—

(BRANDY *tries to get at* STAN *but* RIP *prevents her.* STAN *is so drugged that he must concentrate on standing.* BRANDY *struggles violently in* RIP's *grip.*)

BRANDY: I'll kill that bastard!

RIP: Now, honey—

BRANDY: I'll kill him!

RIP: Shhh—

BRANDY: I won't shut up! What's with the vise-grip? I thought you were a man but you're just a chump. Let a guy who busted up your woman stand there scot free! You should be battering his brain!

RIP: I am.

BRANDY: Messing his mind!

RIP: I have.

BRANDY: You said you'd fix him good so he don't hurt me no more!

RIP: I will.

BRANDY: How?

RIP: I'm charging his battery.

BRANDY: (*Breaking away from* RIP.) I'm charging him *with* battery. Assault and battery.

RIP: Brandy—

BRANDY: Assault and battery! And I got the bruises to prove it. If you don't do something, I sure the hell will.

RIP: Please, baby, don't overheat your engine. Pop off your water top.

BRANDY: My daddy was a hog-butcher, and if it's one thing I know it's how to slice a pig to pieces, and I'm frying his bacon legally. Count on it, buddy-boy.

(BRANDY *begins to leave;* RIP *blocks her path.*)

RIP: Simmer. Turn down the blue gas flame.

BRANDY: Get out of my way.

RIP: Flip on your park lights for a second.

BRANDY: I'm flying to the police station.

Act Two

RIP: Do you love me?

BRANDY: You ain't shovin' that bull in my face again.

RIP: Just answer a question then. What are you doing tonight?

BRANDY: Asshole.

RIP: What are you doing?

BRANDY: Nothing with you.

RIP: I thought we'd rev up and walk through the city obese. Gorge on lobster, liquor, laughs, and gluttonous love. Put on some pounds together.

BRANDY: No.

RIP: A shot of love is the best medicine. I'm gonna give you the whole treatment. I got the evening all planned. To a tee. Soothe your bruise. Doctor's orders. Do I polish my chrome? We get fat tonight or no?

BRANDY: I don't know.

RIP: Just me and you.

BRANDY: No him?

RIP: Alone. Together.

BRANDY: But what about—

RIP: Shhh . . .

BRANDY: Pump Room?

RIP: Only the best for you.

BRANDY: You punk. (*They embrace.*)

RIP: Alright. But before you weld the ball and chain on old Stan and stuff him into a dungeon, you're forcing me to show you something. Come here, Stan. (STAN *moves toward him and collapses onto the worktable.* RIP *lays him down.*)

BRANDY: What's wrong with him? Is he junked up? Didn't know he was a hophead.

RIP: (*Placing the electrodes on* STAN.) This is how I'm sticking up for you. Revenge in the positive. Modern exorcism. To extract what the ancients perceived as the devil. Take the mad out of madman. Erase the first letter 'a' in the word 'Satan' and leave the name 'Stan'.

BRANDY: I don't know what you're talking about.

RIP: In the past, madmen were outcasts. Sent to leper colonies to become outwardly diseased when they were internally sick. Now Man has invented the cure.

BRANDY: What are you doing?

RIP: Perceive. Experience. Transcend. Take a look at a modern miracle. Magic without illusion. A new faith. Purge bad blood with electric transfusion. Transubstantiation.

(RIP *turns on the ECT device.*)

BRANDY: (*Quietly*) Oh my God.

BLACKOUT

Scene 2

(*Two weeks later.* RIP *and* STAN *are working.* STAN *wears no bandages. He looks at* RIP *as if to say something, stops himself and goes back to work. He is all incomplete gestures. Finally, he speaks.*)

STAN: What, it's been two weeks? (*Pause*) Two weeks ago was the Ice Age. Glaciers. Darkness. Novacaine brain. Numb skull. But the ice has melted. The sun's out now and everything's in bloom. I'm here. Myself. Truly. I'm not shot full of fear. No terror. No worry about what my hands are gonna do. The rage when someone looks at you funny. Tense. Tight.

ACT TWO 49

RIP: Got to relax, Stan. Adjust your idle to a lower level.

STAN: If I adjust any lower, I'd *be* idle. I've never been so relaxed. Thanks to you, Rip. I've been feeling so, I don't know, good, great, that I use my time more. It's exciting. I'm thinking of things outside myself. Not just me. I'm not just an engine running inside a chest. Some engine on automatic pilot. Just living. I'm thinking. I'm looking. I'm not just (*Acting fearful*) looking out. I'm (*Confident and searching*) looking out. I've been thinking. Really thinking. Light bulbs over my head. Light bulbs. And I've been dying to tell you something. I'm butterflies just thinking of your reaction. I want you to be proud of me, Rip. So bad. Like an ache. Want to be really part of you. A working part of your jigsaw. So I guess I shoot. Check this. The electronic component design for Whitehall? The problem of two-step punching through the phone? Elephant-ear this. (*Pause*) An 80-86 chip. Place it right into the phone. You get a myriad of number combos. A whole phone control center running the other systems throughout the house. The system uses less energy than your blueprint. More expensive but more convenient. Your doctrine. The rich pay for simplicity. And it makes your punch-system one step. Ta-da! But more important, I thought of it. Me. (*Pause*) Well? What do you think? I'm hanging on a thread.

RIP: Too late.

STAN: What?

RIP: Too late. I'm going with my original.

STAN: What do you mean too late?

RIP: Just what I said. Run across the street for some coffee, will ya, buddy-boy? Double sugar. Get a cup for yourself. I'll pop for it.

STAN: I don't get it.

RIP: You get it. You get coffee. That's what you get. (*Pause*) No go. It's not feasible.

STAN: Why?

RIP: Don't ask why. (*Pause*) Doesn't make sense.

STAN: It makes perfect sense. And it's so simple. I don't know why you didn't think of it.

RIP: Hey. Headlights off and pull your emergency.

STAN: Why don't you go for it?

RIP: Go for it? I'm no gopher. I don't go for nothing. You go for it. Black. Double sugar. You reorganized the tools. I can't find anything.

STAN: It's more efficient. But why?

RIP: Stan, never ask why. Only ask me how.

STAN: Why?

RIP: What did I just say?

STAN: Then how?

RIP: By not asking. I tell you. You don't do me. Capiche?

STAN: Why? I mean how?

RIP: By getting coffee.

BLACKOUT

Scene 3

(*One week later.* RIP *and* BRANDY *are drinking boilermakers.* BRANDY *cracks one egg into each of the two glasses of beer.*)

BRANDY: Nothing like sitting down to a good meal.

(BRANDY *slugs a shot of Jack Daniels whiskey and drinks from the beer.*)

ACT TWO

RIP: (*Flatly*) Yeah.

BRANDY: (*Imitating him.*) Yeah.

RIP: (*Irritably.*) I said yeah.

BRANDY: Okay, okay. Just trying to liven up this party, pumpkin. You look like you just lost your best friend.

RIP: I think I have.

BRANDY: I don't want to hear about that retard! I dropped the battery charge against him on the condition we don't talk about that psycho. Knowing he's bananas is worse than what I thought of him before. It don't make me more sympathetic, it makes him more of a weirdo. And here I am talking about him after I just said we ain't talking about that spook. Now that's final. No sickos. Let's put on some music. Dance music.

(BRANDY *turns on the radio and dances.* RIP *goes to turn the radio off, but she intercepts him.*)

RIP: I got to turn it off. He's asleep.

BRANDY: What's he doing here?

RIP: He's bedding down here during treatment.

BRANDY: Your monster has moved in with us. Perfect. Well, turn it down not off. Loony tunes can compromise that.

RIP: Alright. (*He turns down the radio.*)

BRANDY: Wanna shoot a beer?

RIP: Greasy kid stuff. Like slicking your D.A.

BRANDY: A little dab'll do me. (RIP *takes a long drink.*) You in a coma or what? I just wanna brown your toast, flip your eggs, and get your coffee perking, darlin'. (*Throwing her arms around him.*) All right. What's wrong? Don't tell me it's the crucified mental case with a crown of electrodes.

RIP: It's been three weeks at three shocks a week. That should be the end of the treatment. But he's not the way I expected him to be. He's telling me what to do. We both get into moods. I feel unsure. Scrambled. I don't know. What am I nuts?

BRANDY: Well, you got to admit that the idea to hook him up in here like some kind of car battery is a scene from the Twilight Zone.

RIP: Shut-up. You're right. No more talk about him. I'm finished. And so is this music. Gets on my nerves. (*He unplugs the radio.*) I need help. I need a third eye.

BRANDY: Thought we were done talking about demento.

RIP: I want you to jaw with Stan a lick.

BRANDY: I'll lick him in the jaw with brass knuckles.

RIP: Nobody can know about this treatment. You're the only one. I'm too close to the therapy. I can't trust my own eyes. It's got to be you. I just want you to talk with him. Test his memory. See if he's changed and tell me that he's himself, the same old Stan. That I did the right thing. That I'm still in control. Talk to him.

BRANDY: No.

RIP: I'm asking you.

BRANDY: No.

RIP: Then I'm telling you.

BRANDY: You're what?

RIP: I'm telling you what to do.

BRANDY: You don't tell me nothing.

RIP: He won't attack you. I guarantee. Don't be afraid of getting hit.

BRANDY: I'm not. He just surprised me, that's all. Here. (*She pushes his beer toward him.*) Suck this down and sink back into a coma.

ACT TWO 53

RIP: You'll do what I say. You talk to Stan. Give me your impression of him.

BRANDY: I'll impress his face with the flat of my hand.

RIP: Do it.

BRANDY: No.

RIP: Do what I say.

BRANDY: No, damnit.

RIP: Do it.

BRANDY: No.

RIP: Do what I say.

(RIP *slaps* BRANDY *in the face.*)

BLACKOUT

Scene 4

(*The next day.* STAN *works on a blueprint.* BRANDY *knocks.*)

STAN: Come in. (BRANDY *enters.*) Hello.

BRANDY: Hello.

STAN: Rip's not here. He's—

BRANDY: I know.

STAN: Oh.

BRANDY: Mind if I stay awhile?

STAN: Well. Sure. Not if you don't mind me finishing up on this blueprint. My first systems idea.

BRANDY: Don't mind me.

STAN: We can still talk. Would you like a drink? (*Pause*) Drambuie?

BRANDY: You kidding? This early? That's an after-dinner anyways.

STAN: Pardon me?

BRANDY: It's a liqueur.

STAN: What is?

BRANDY: Forget it.

STAN: You sure? How about a Mountain Dew?

BRANDY: That's more like it. If you got one. (STAN *gets the soda and gives it to her.*) You remembered my drink. (*Baitingly*) How do you feel?

STAN: Fine. And you?

BRANDY: Fine. (*Pause*) I mean. How has the treatment affected you?

STAN: You know about that?

BRANDY: Of course.

STAN: Oh.

BRANDY: Your memory?

STAN: Great. (*Pause*) Drambuie, I—

BRANDY: I said no. I'm already drinking a pop.

STAN: What?

BRANDY: Your memory's fine but you're deaf. I said no.

STAN: No what?

BRANDY: No thanks.

(*Pause*)

STAN: Do you really want to know how I feel after the treatment?

BRANDY: I said I did.

STAN: I own my eyes. Truly. My own eyes. I trust them. My irises have bloomed. Before I was a pupil looking for a teacher, now my own eye pupil teaches me.

ACT TWO

BRANDY: What does your pupil teach you?

STAN: To see things clearly. As they are. And not to look away.

BRANDY: What aren't you looking away from?

STAN: You.

BRANDY: Me?

STAN: You. Drambuie.

BRANDY: You got Drambuie on the brain.

STAN: And in my eyes. Drambuie: a woman that boils the blood. Sweet but with a kick.

BRANDY: My name's Drambuie.

STAN: No introduction. I see you.

BRANDY: And what do you see?

STAN: A woman with smarts.

BRANDY: You're bent in more ways than one. No one's said I got smarts from the moment I came screaming out of my mamma's womb. That's how busted down your jalopy of a brain is.

STAN: My old junk's been repaired to brand-spanking new. You have the smarts to become more than you're letting yourself be. You don't have faith in yourself. You're mistreated.

BRANDY: That's a joke coming from you.

STAN: You've been getting the wrong type of treatment.

BRANDY: Listen, clown, don't make me laugh.

STAN: See the treatment you're receiving as a physical matter. A force to be accepted or rejected. Since you've accepted this treatment, it's up to you how to use it from there. Let it open your eyes like mine. Don't settle for the mold someone else designs. Design your own blueprint. You have heart like me.

BRANDY: You're a laugh riot, Chuckles.

STAN: I'm serious.

BRANDY: And I'm looking at a bad sight gag right between the eyes.

STAN: I'm looking at a brain with a heart. No joke.

BRANDY: Yeah? If you're such an egghead, what do you think of a lug who beats up on a woman?

STAN: A painful treatment. And wrong. But what does she do next? Do you have a specific case?

BRANDY: Don't act sly. Alright. I'll play along. I got a local joke for you. There's this chick and there's this dunce. That's the set-up. Ready for the punchline? The dunce hauls off and smashes the woman in the face. Get it? Funny stuff, huh?

STAN: I think that—

BRANDY: You think what, brain box?

STAN: I'd say—

BRANDY: I'd say you need a little more clown white under your eyes.

STAN: Really? I just touched them up a minute ago.

BRANDY: You just missed your train of thought, comedian. Must run on a schedule.

STAN: My train's on detour. Several tracks run through my mind.

BRANDY: And they all need repairs.

STAN: Excuse me. Be right back. Gotta strap on my red nose.

BRANDY: Listen, Emmett. (*Pause*) The masquerade's over. I got the cold cream that's gonna strip your greasepaint. I want you barefaced, buster. The midnight chime just came down on Halloween.

STAN: Then it's All Saints' Day.

BRANDY: And I'm a saint not to rip your head off.

STAN: Why are you yelling at me? You say you're a saint; can't you say you're the woman who was hit?

BRANDY: Can't you say you're the one who hit me?

STAN: I hit you?

BRANDY: Bingo, bozo.

STAN: What?

BRANDY: See this bruise?

STAN: Yeah.

BRANDY: It's faded. But as I've been talking with you, it's flared up, like the bruise feels your presence. My whole eye is throbbing. It must be as purple now as the morning after you screwed your fist into my face.

STAN: I don't understand. I didn't bruise you.

BRANDY: Then I don't have a bruise.

STAN: But you do.

BRANDY: Then you did.

(*Pause*)

STAN: Okay. Let's slow down the ping-pong. Why would I attack a woman like you who I consider it a privilege just to speak with?

BRANDY: Because you're a mental case. Crackers.

STAN: You were hit before my treatment?

BRANDY: That's why Rip gave you the treatment, idiot.

STAN: Because I beat you?

BRANDY: Am I talking to the ceiling?

(*Pause.* STAN *pulls out a large monkey wrench and approaches* BRANDY. *He kneels and offers her the wrench.*)

STAN: Here. Smash me in the head with this. Don't think about it. Just do it. An eye for an eye. (*She grabs the wrench from him.*) Hit me. (*Pause. She drops it to the floor. He picks it up and aims it at his head.*) Give me the word and I'll do it.

BRANDY: I wish I knew you.

STAN: You know me by what I do.

BRANDY: Put it down.

(STAN *puts down the wrench.*)

STAN: You forgive me?

BRANDY: I don't know.

(*Silence*)

STAN: Take this as a peace offering. (*He offers her a metal nut.*) Carry it with you. Everytime you put your hand in your pocket, you'll remember me. Remember that I'm deeply sorry for everything I've done to you. A nut from a nut. (*She takes the nut and begins to leave.*) Will you see me tomorrow?

BRANDY: Maybe.

STAN: Tomorrow then.

(BRANDY *exits.*)

BLACKOUT

Scene 5

(*The following morning.* RIP *and* STAN *are working.*)

RIP: So this is the meanest cat you ever had the terror of being scratched by. A Siamese if you please. The cat was completely out of his mind. Well, one night the chick and I are watching T.V. when sparks start flying from the back of the set. I jump up, run around to the back of the box and there's the cat with his lips curled back, his teeth locked around the extension cord, electricity bolting through its body, flipping back and forth like a living cartoon. I yank the cat off the wire and throw him across the room. He shakes his head and inches away in slow motion. He sits under a chair for literally two days. I begin getting worried. Then all of a sudden he was fine. Calmest cat in the world from then on. Funniest thing I ever saw. Give me a screwdriver, will ya? (STAN *gets the tool*.) Hey! I was talking to my little fur trap last night. Said she had a talk with you. Said you're getting along terrific. Just like you were before all this, but better.

STAN: Did she.

RIP: Yeah. I feel great you feel great. You're everything to me, Stan. Ah, I don't have to tell you that. I think one more treatment and you're a cured man. As free as a souped-up Lotus flying down the highway eating up white lines.

STAN: I think I'm okay now.

RIP: I said one more. I felt so fantastic after Brandy told me you were up to your oats that I opened her trunk and threw in my spare. Jacked her up 'til she honked. That little girl's great in the bunk. Probably why I keep her around. What a broad.

STAN: Don't talk about her like that.

RIP: What?

STAN: Don't talk about her like that.

(*Pause*)

RIP: Don't talk about my bumper how I want to talk about her?

STAN: Forget it.

RIP: You forget it.

STAN: I'll forget it.

RIP: You better forget it.

STAN: Forget it.

RIP: Forget it. (*Pause*) Let's never have a broad come between us. Not between buddies. (*Pause*) Unless we're screwing her at the same time. (*He reaches for a wire.*)

STAN: Watch out that's a live—

RIP: (*Getting shocked.*) Owww!

STAN: Wire.

RIP: You got me messed with your talk.

STAN: Sorry.

RIP: I never get shocked.

STAN: Can't say never no more.

RIP: I'll say never if I want to. Don't tell me what to do. I never get shocked. I don't need to get shocked. I'm not nuts. I never get shocked and I never will.

BLACKOUT

Scene 6

(*Later that same day. A suitcase stands by the worktable.* STAN *places some tools and his blueprint into a sack. He does not wear his work shirt but buttons up a casual one. There is a knock at the door.*)

STAN: Who is it?

BRANDY: (*Offstage*) It's me.

STAN: Just a minute.

(*He straps on a red clown nose and unlocks the door.* BRANDY *enters, offering a bottle of Drambuie.*)

BRANDY: Like some Drambuie, clownie? (*They laugh. She is dressed attractively but not in an overtly sexual way.*)

STAN: We both took a chance on that one.

BRANDY: You're telling me.

STAN: I'll get some glasses. Straight or on the rocks?

BRANDY: We've been on the rocks. Let's pour straight.

STAN: We really broke the ice.

(BRANDY *pours the Drambuie. They click their glasses and drink.*)

BRANDY: Sweet.

STAN: A kick.

BRANDY: (*Noticing the suitcase.*) You moving back to your apartment?

STAN: Nope.

BRANDY: Where you going?

STAN: Away.

BRANDY: Out of town?

STAN: Way out of town.

BRANDY: Vacation?

STAN: Permanent.

BRANDY: Oh. Came on kinda sudden.

STAN: Overdue.

BRANDY: Why?

STAN: Your question is the answer. Why is because of why. Why does electricity work? I know how but I want to know why. A lot of people are hows. Rip's a how. That's fine. But I'm a why. I don't care how an engine runs, I want to know—

BOTH: Why. (*They laugh.*)

STAN: I'd like to study physics instead of mechanics. Maybe I can teach myself. I have a good pupil now.

BRANDY: What town you heading to?

STAN: Houston, Texas. Figure I'll start from the bottom of the country and work my way up. It's a brand new city, full of new ideas.

(BRANDY *pours more drinks.*)

BRANDY: There's something you said yesterday that hit me like a lightning storm. About the treatment I've been getting. How I can take it or leave it. You may be nuts but you ain't stupid. (*Pause*) I don't know. Something's gotta change. I feel like I'm on the verge of something but I don't know what. (*Pause*) You ever feel like you understand everything at once but you can't say what it is?

STAN: Yeah. Like you can only chip away at it.

BRANDY: Yeah. (*Pause*) It's weird. Like I don't have my own blood in my body. Like someone else is pushing the buttons. I'm being operated. A machine. Bloodless.

STAN: That's how I am. Was. Not now. Now I have my own blood.

BRANDY: So should I. Will. I gotta get my own blood pumping through me.

STAN: Lately I don't think I have blood at all. It's champagne bubbling through my veins. (*Pause*) Oh, yeah. Talk about wacko. I remembered that your name's not—

DRAMBUIE: My name's Drambuie.

(*Pause*)

EMMETT: Like I said. Drambuie. Well, Drambuie, I'd like to introduce myself. The name's Emmett.

(*They shake hands and laugh.*)

DRAMBUIE: Glad to meet you, Emmett. Goddamn glad.

(*They click their glasses and drink.*)

EMMETT: Now I gotta go. (*He moves away.*)

DRAMBUIE: Go?

EMMETT: Yeah.

DRAMBUIE: Now?

EMMETT: Before Rip—

DRAMBUIE: One more.

EMMETT: Can't. Say goodbye to him—

DRAMBUIE: Like to talk to you more about—See, I can't just hook myself up to a treat machine.

EMMETT: We didn't talk forever, now we don't have the time.

DRAMBUIE: But—

EMMETT: Besides, the more I drink this stuff, the redder my nose gets.

DRAMBUIE: Redder than Harlequin.

EMMETT: That's right. Pierrot nose.

DRAMBUIE: Punchinello nose.

EMMETT: Punched nose.

DRAMBUIE: Bloody nose. I've got enough of those. That's my inheritance. Blood nose.

EMMETT: Blue nose.

DRAMBUIE: Blue blood.

EMMETT: Royal blood.

DRAMBUIE: Bloodline.

EMMETT: To pass blood.

DRAMBUIE: Let blood.

EMMETT: Give blood.

DRAMBUIE: Take blood.

EMMETT: Transfusion.
DRAMBUIE: Vampire.
EMMETT: Feed from each other.
DRAMBUIE: Live off each other.
EMMETT: Nourish each other.
DRAMBUIE: Cultivate.
EMMETT: Plant.
DRAMBUIE: Seed.
EMMETT: Germ.
DRAMBUIE: Kernel.
EMMETT: Harvest.
DRAMBUIE: Thanksgiving.
EMMETT: Ritual.
DRAMBUIE: Communion.
EMMETT: Confessional.
DRAMBUIE: Penance.
EMMETT: Stigmata.
DRAMBUIE: Crucify.
EMMETT: Martyr.
DRAMBUIE: Saint.
EMMETT: Miracles.
DRAMBUIE: Voices.
EMMETT: Premonitions.
DRAMBUIE: Visions.
EMMETT: Mega-dreams.
DRAMBUIE: Super-hopes.
EMMETT: Power-concepts.

Act Two

DRAMBUIE: Idea to reality.
EMMETT: Brain to matter.
DRAMBUIE: Dust to dust.
EMMETT: Death.
DRAMBUIE: Ashes to ashes.
EMMETT: Life.
DRAMBUIE: Birth to rebirth.
EMMETT: Love.
DRAMBUIE: Mind to mind.
EMMETT: Flesh to flesh.
DRAMBUIE: Hand to hand.
EMMETT: Lip to lip.
DRAMBUIE: Breast to chest.
EMMETT: Eye to eye.
DRAMBUIE: Equal.
EMMETT: Even match.
DRAMBUIE: Brain-erection.
EMMETT: Mind-penetration.
DRAMBUIE: Passion.
EMMETT: Union.
DRAMBUIE: Clinch.
EMMETT: Life-force.
DRAMBUIE: Tender.
EMMETT: Gentle.
DRAMBUIE: Soft.
EMMETT: Smooth emotion.
DRAMBUIE: Ocean of emotion.

EMMETT: Emotion motion.

DRAMBUIE: Inner movement.

EMMETT: Internal change.

DRAMBUIE: Muscle metamorphosis.

EMMETT: Reorganized organs.

DRAMBUIE: Sever.

EMMETT: Cut.

DRAMBUIE: Break away.

EMMETT: Leave.

DRAMBUIE: (*With emphasis*) Rip. Apart.

EMMETT: Clean break.

DRAMBUIE: Inner cleansing.

EMMETT: Soul enema.

DRAMBUIE: Pure heart.

EMMETT: You have heart.

DRAMBUIE: You.

EMMETT: Me.

DRAMBUIE: Me.

EMMETT: You.

DRAMBUIE: Us.

EMMETT: Us.

DRAMBUIE: Heart.

EMMETT: Blood pump.

DRAMBUIE: Bloodline.

EMMETT: Pass on.

DRAMBUIE: Carry on.

EMMETT: Give birth.

DRAMBUIE: Conceive.

EMMETT: Create.

DRAMBUIE: Family tree.

EMMETT: Generation.

DRAMBUIE: Spirit.

EMMETT: Hope.

DRAMBUIE: Dreams.

EMMETT: Future.

DRAMBUIE: Past.

EMMETT: Blood.

DRAMBUIE: My blood.

EMMETT: Your blood.

DRAMBUIE: Spill blood.

EMMETT: Blood brothers.

(EMMETT *cuts his finger with a penknife. He offers his finger to* DRAMBUIE. *She puts her mouth on his finger. Pause. She wraps his finger in a tissue. They look at each other for a while.*)

DRAMBUIE: (*Suddenly*) What the hell just happened?

EMMETT: I don't know.

DRAMBUIE: Are we married or something?

EMMETT: I really don't know.

DRAMBUIE: Electroshock can't be nothing compared to that.

EMMETT: Like we were speaking a different language.

DRAMBUIE: Tongues or something.

EMMETT: What a brain lock.

DRAMBUIE: But it felt good.

EMMETT: Felt great. (*Pause*) You messed with my finger, I want to mess with yours. Give me your hand. (*He takes out a ring and holds her hand.*) This is an 80-86 chip. It's also the first idea I had on my own. The chip is welded onto a silver band. Of all substances, silver is the most conductive to electricity. I figure if you're wearing silver, I can get through to you easier. The chip runs on its own energy like a battery. But a one-celled battery. Able to self-generate. Whole within itself. Though this chip is small, it has devastating possibilities. Because it's tiny, it seems simple. But it can add, subtract, multiply, divide, give the date, the weather, sound alarms, deal with the stars. It even has a good memory. It's a complex little mechanism. If you only give it a quick glance, it looks like a piece of junk. I could give you a—

DRAMBUIE: I want this.

(*He slips the ring on her finger. They kiss.*)

EMMETT: Our lips fit together perfectly. (*Silence. They look into each other's eyes.*) But I still gotta go.

DRAMBUIE: Me, too. On my own. I can't lose myself in you right now.

EMMETT: Our timing's been all off.

DRAMBUIE: Will you keep in touch, just so I know where you are?

EMMETT: I will. Yeah. (*Pause*) Okay. Now I really gotta go. I mean, you know, Rip, ah, anyway, I'm in a rush now, see. You wait around your whole life for something to happen, then when you finally move out on our own, you're speeding so fast you can hardly keep up with yourself.

DRAMBUIE: You ain't even gonna say goodbye to him?

EMMETT: If I say goodbye, I might not leave. I gotta go.

DRAMBUIE: You can do it. Good luck.

ACT TWO

EMMETT: You can, too. Stand up to it.

DRAMBUIE: Give yourself the whole treatment.

(*They hug. While they are separating from the hug,* RIP *enters.*)

RIP: Pretty cozy, you two. What's rocking? What's the buzz behind my back? Throwing crumbs to the dogs, Brandy? Now what could you two be talking about without me? Or are we just playing doctor? Give me your best shot, nurse. Slip me your mickey, knock me out with a sip of spiked Brandy. Come here, baby.

DRAMBUIE: No.

RIP: Ah. This is complicated.

EMMETT: Drambuie.

RIP: Say what?

EMMETT: Hold tight, Drambuie.

RIP: Say what, what? What you call her? You don't tell her nothing, Stan. She'll hold tight. To me. Like she's clenched to a revved-up hog blasting down the alley. And her name's Brandy.

DRAMBUIE: My name's Drambuie.

RIP: Therapeutic? Fine, darlin'. He can call you whatever he wants. Ding-dong, Poopsie, Bozo, I don't care. But I'm here now. You get over here, sweetmeats, and plant one on me. Give me some sugar. Your man. The bes' of the mess.

DRAMBUIE: I ain't your woman no more.

RIP: I know you ain't my woman. You're my little girl. Now get over here before I spank you.

DRAMBUIE: Greasemonkey.

RIP: Roughhouse? I'm up for it. You're a stick shift, I'll slam you into gear.

DRAMBUIE: You always got your head stuck under a hood. You care less about me than a carburetor. You don't think I know that? I'll make this short and sweet, Rip. Let me spell it out nice and clear. Read my lips, pal. You are incapable of true love. I'm leaving you.

EMMETT: Bleed.

DRAMBUIE: Blood to blood.

EMMETT: Cut the cord.

DRAMBUIE: Break the safe.

EMMETT: Adapt.

DRAMBUIE: Change.

RIP: You two just take a trip to Mars? (*Pause*) What the hell was that? You ask Stan if I can love. And what's that piece of junk on your finger?

DRAMBUIE: I'm walking out. By myself. So's Emmett.

RIP: What's an emmett?

DRAMBUIE: I'm leaving you! Got it? Get it. Good. (*Pause*) And Emmett's a guy who's got his own blood in his veins.

RIP: He's not dead meat. Good. I can arrange that. Stan, you know this guy Emmett?

EMMETT: I'm leaving, too.

(*Silence*)

RIP: Those your bags?

EMMETT: Yeah.

RIP: Uh-huh. Okay. I get it. Emmett.

DRAMBUIE: Chip the shell.

EMMETT: Crack the boundary.

DRAMBUIE: Cross borders.

EMMETT: Smash barriers.

RIP: Shut-up! Talk my language. Machines.

DRAMBUIE: Blood.

RIP: Electricity.

EMMETT: Heart.

RIP: Voltage.

DRAMBUIE: Heat.

RIP: Amperage.

EMMETT: Bloodbeat.

RIP: Watts.

DRAMBUIE: Throb.

RIP: Horsepower.

EMMETT: Pulse.

RIP: (*Shoving* EMMETT *up against a wall.*) Nobody jumps my bumper. Not you. Not nobody. Get off her.

DRAMBUIE: Me and Emmett ain't leaving together.

RIP: You think I'm blind? That I didn't see what I saw?

DRAMBUIE: It ain't that simple.

RIP: There's got to be someone else.

(DRAMBUIE *tries to pull* RIP *away from* EMMETT. RIP *pushes her away releasing* EMMETT.)

DRAMBUIE: I ain't leaving 'cause of someone else. I'm leaving for me. Can't you get it through your skull? It ain't somebody else. It's you.

(*Pause*)

EMMETT: I gotta go.

RIP: That's impossible. I can't release you, Stan. Not without post-shock therapy. Not until your adaptation is complete. To leave now is out of the question.

EMMETT: I'll take that chance.

RIP: I'm afraid of what'll happen to you out there. How will you protect yourself? How you gonna eat? You can't even fix a radio.

EMMETT: I'll be fine.

RIP: You can't tune a car.

EMMETT: I'm going to Houston.

RIP: It's the wrong time, Stan. I've got so much to teach you. Worlds to learn. Thousands of things you don't know. Concepts only I can explain. Techniques I want to pass on to you. Short-cuts. Methods. System designs. I'll give you everything. You can take me apart piece by piece.

EMMETT: I want to study physics.

RIP: Go partners with me. Fifty-fifty. Straight down the middle. Equal power. Me and you. Even-steven. Design whatever you want. You're the boss.

(*Pause*)

EMMETT: I'm leaving. (*Pause*) You've given me so much, Rip. You busted me out of a cell. But I gotta go. On my own. I gotta. (*Pause*) If you wanna give me something, give me your approval. I still depend on that. I want your blessing. I want to carry it with me. (*Pause*) I want you to want me to go.

(*Pause*)

RIP: I love you, Brandy. (*Pause*) If I didn't act the way I did, if I wasn't the way I am, you would've never fallen in love with me. You know that. You love what I am. (*Pause*) I've never taken to anyone like I do you, Stan. (*Pause*) If you both leave, this shop is empty. Just a bunch of broken stuff. I fix things. Maybe 'cause there's something busted in me. I need something to.... I need you. Don't leave. Don't bust the battery.

ACT TWO

(*Silence*)

DRAMBUIE: I gotta go.

EMMETT: I'm going.

DRAMBUIE: We had something, Rip. Sometimes even a little piece of heaven. But there's gotta be something more. If something doesn't move, you wonder if it's alive. I know what tomorrow is with you. I gotta find my world. Can you understand that? Can you wish me luck? (*Pause*) Rip, are you alright? (*Pause*) Treat yourself good, Emmett. Bye, Rip.

(DRAMBUIE *exits.*)

RIP: Why—I mean, how. How did this. How did you.

EMMETT: I gotta go.

RIP: How?

EMMETT: I'll never be able to pay you back.

RIP: I mean why.

EMMETT: You're okay, Rip. You can make it. Aces.

RIP: Why?

EMMETT: Aces.

RIP: Why?

EMMETT: Aces.

(EMMETT *exits.*)

RIP: Why?

BLACKOUT

End of the Play

Property List

Worktable:

Coffee pot
Cup
Sugar
Electrical tape
Battery tester
Long-nose pliers
Screwdrivers
Terminal connector
Can of pencils
Radio

Under Table:

Paper towels
Soldering iron
Screwdriver
Large circuit for RIP
Blueprint plans
Wrench
Nut
First-aid box
alcohol
cotton
gel
two syringes
hydrogen peroxide
gauze
medical tape
scissors
head bandage
Towel for STAN
Empty Coke bottle

Rip's *Desk:*

Treat Machine
Telephone
Newspaper
Garbage can
Briefcase
Adding machine
Mail

Shelves:

Iron
Toaster
Batteries in Bin

Stan's *Desk*:

Bagel in bag
Aspirin
Screwdriver
Lamp
Garbage can

Prop Table (Offstage):

Almost empty Coke bottle
Two eggs
Two beers
Two empty beers
Two mugs
Two shot glasses
Bottle of tabasco (tomato juice)
Salt
Pepper
Half-full bottle Jack Daniels
    Bourbon

Personal:

Rip:
  Blueprint plans
  Keys
  Money

Stan:
  Nut
  Ring
  Penknife
  Ace bandage

Brandy:
  Address on slip of paper
  Drambuie

Refrigerator:

Three Cokes
One Mountain Dew (water)
Bottle opener

www.ingramcontent.com/pod-product-compliance
Lightning Source LLC
Chambersburg PA
CBHW060215050426
42446CB00013B/3073